Educating
Ha.nh

KATHLEEN HAMILTON

◆ FriesenPress

Suite 300 - 990 Fort St
Victoria, BC, V8V 3K2
Canada

www.friesenpress.com

Copyright © 2017 by Kathleen Hamilton
First Edition — 2017

All rights reserved.

No part of this publication may be reproduced in any form, or by any means, electronic or mechanical, including photocopying, recording, or any information browsing, storage, or retrieval system, without permission in writing from FriesenPress.

ISBN
978-1-5255-0173-9 (Hardcover)
978-1-5255-0174-6 (Paperback)
978-1-5255-0175-3 (eBook)

1. Biography & Autobiography, Educators

Distributed to the trade by The Ingram Book Company

A special thank you to Holly Baines;
my Royal Roads University Advisor.

Educating Hạnh

VIETNAMESE CALLED IT THE AMERICAN WAR, while the west called it the Vietnamese War. Co^ng called it *dia nguc*. It was a living, breathing hell. At sixteen her life was broken, without purpose. Her village was a skeleton, shattered into many splinters; forms without familiarity. There were no longer neat paths between houses. No longer were there proudly kept houses lined with vegetable gardens. Gone was the freedom to enjoy a few moments of bliss in a hard working day. Like watercolours on a saturated canvas, days ran into months. But there was no time for boredom, each moment had to be one of alertness, watching for the ever present danger, the danger that shattered the silence. Of course, there were the natural dangers; poisonous snakes, scorpions, tuberculosis, and common illnesses, but now there were the dangers of both them and the other ones.

Co^ng was afraid of them. Co^ng was angry with them. Co^ng hated them. It had been them who had tortured her father, and destroyed his spirit. It was them who had taken her brothers, Minh, Sa'ng, and Quo^'c. With tears streaming down their bloody cheeks, Minh and Sa'ng had, without choice, followed the Vietcong, the North Vietnamese army, to war after a brief scuffle. Quo^'c had refused, and this was taken by the Vietcong soldiers as an admission that he sided with the south; with the other ones. He had been an example in the village centre for all to see; stripped, tortured, and finally hung over a pool of his blood on his last remaining breath. He had been determined, a freedom fighter, a lover of peace. This child of peace had died defending his cause, the cause of peace, thought of by many to be the cause of South Vietnam, the cause of the other ones. This child had only been fifteen years old.

Co^ng had covered her sister's eyes from the horror. She had always tried to protect Ha.nh. As the eldest sister that was her job, and Ha.nh would have put herself and Co^ng in danger. Ha.nh was fourteen years old and her beauty radiated in a world gone terribly wrong. At that time, being born female in Vietnam was an immediate disadvantage. Aside from not being the sought after male child, there was neither equality, nor freedom, and being beautiful put a girl in imminent danger – especially now when soldiers were amongst them. Soldiers took but never gave; food, beds, girls for pleasure, and boys for war.

In the darkness preceding the new dawn, Co^ng and her sister rose before their mother, Ngo^n. They rose before the American soldiers, the men who had recently entered their village to protect them, or so they were told, to begin their chores, prepare breakfast, and leave their house for safety at the house of Auntie Dung. Co^ng always trusted her mother and never disobeyed, for all she wanted was to feel safe, a feeling that she would not truly feel for a very long time, perhaps a lifetime.

After a simple meal of watered down rice porridge, Co^ng and Ha.nh quietly crept through the village, to the single flickering candle in Auntie Dung's window. Twelve more steps; the daily routine was clocked in steps. Fifty-nine total, only twelve to go, but on that day those twelve steps would not come. And as Co^ng and Ha.nh lay gagged, suffocating on the sandy forest floor they wished for only death, something that would not happen that day. Too soon for one, but it was not that day.

The American war ended the following year to the first cry of a baby, and the last breath of a broken girl, a mother who had lost her innocence, her dreams, her mother's love, her chance at life. Co^ng held the newborn close as she watched Ha.nh being prepared for burial.

Minh had returned from the war without his legs, carried by Sa'ng who was weakened and slowly dying from tuberculosis. Sa'ng was now bedridden. Minh was good with his hands, doing the best he could to help rebuild their shattered past. Of the many boys who had been drafted into war, few returned to take their places in the patriarchal society, the society that had been put on hold in their absence, temporarily reshaped by women. Father was waiting at the welcome mat of death's door. Co^ng was now mother to four. At forty-two years her mother, the grey haired Ngo^n, was only a shell, unable to care for her weakened sons, her dying husband, or her granddaughter. So she sat by the fire in a stupor, mourning her losses. Co^ng prayed to Buddah every day for strength. She named the baby Xuan, "spring", because she was born as the war ended, bringing new life, new hope to a family, broken as those throughout her village; a village of shattered dreams.

The year was 1993, and Co^ng was thirty-four years old. She worked in the rice field with her husband and two sons. Xuan was now eighteen years old, took care of the water buffalo, the house, and kept food on the table for her family. During the afternoons her hands busied themselves at the loom, weaving simple scarves and table cloths of silk for a market in the neighbouring village. And as she sat at the loom, creating depictions of nature and peace, she would dream. What would her life be like if she were able to get an education? Not just learning primary literacy, but a real education? To be able to get away from the rice fields and into the city? Her dream was to have a shop, not a simple roadside shack, but a real shop full of fine silk *ao dai*, the traditional Vietnamese women's dresses. Her fine silks would be known all over Da Nang: the silks of Miss Xuan. And so this dream went for the next seven years. When she confided in her mother Co^ng, she was warned to get her head out of the clouds. There was work to be done and dreams were simply that. It was time to come back down to earth and touch the ground on which she was born. Life was hard, yes mother Co^ng, life was hard. Besides, the next day was the day to travel to see Tuan, who lived with his parents in the neighbouring village. And on that day there was to be a surprise for her.

Xuan and Tuan had been friends since they were toddlers, meeting whenever their mothers went to the Sunday morning market, and as they grew they had played, helped their mothers sell, and opened booths of their own. But this day was to be different, a day of sorrow for Xuan, a day of shattered dreams. Xuan was to marry Tuan at the end of Buddhist lent for it was time for the beginning of the next generation, a generation riding on the shoulders of Xuan – at least for now since her brothers were only ten and twelve. Besides, one was already spoken for, to become a Buddhist monk. As Xuan carried out her chores, and wove her thoughts, she cried. For four days the rivers emptied her dreams. Then it was over. It was time to take her place and do her duty. This was her place. Co^ng had raised her as her own, but had shared with her the horrors of her past, the beauty of Xuan's mother, stories of her ancestors, where she was from, and the dreams that she, Co^ng, had once had.

The year was 2001, and a baby girl was born to Xuan and Tuan. They named her Ha.nh. Xuan and grandmother Co^ng, cried and prayed for their new gift. From Buddah they asked for the courage to dream, good luck, good fortune. For Ha.nh they prayed for fame and fortune; for an education, one beyond the village level of Grade five, one which would enable her to follow her dreams, and her chosen path. It had been a gift foreseen by the village fortune teller. Xuan had been aware of the villagers' faith in the fortune teller from a very young age, and so she was eager to believe the toothless, grey haired, bent man when he told her that Ha.nh would bring great honour to the family. He had gone on to say that she would have great power, although he was unable to surmise how this would come to pass. All he was able to come up with was "great teacher", and since Xuan did not consider any of the teachers of their tiny village "great", she kept watch for a sign. As she wove dreams for her daughter, she gave birth to 2 sons who, while Tuan tried to be non-traditional, were favoured by their father. Xuan wove stronger dreams for she knew that her daughter needed all her strength to help carry the great power.

KATHLEEN HAMILTON

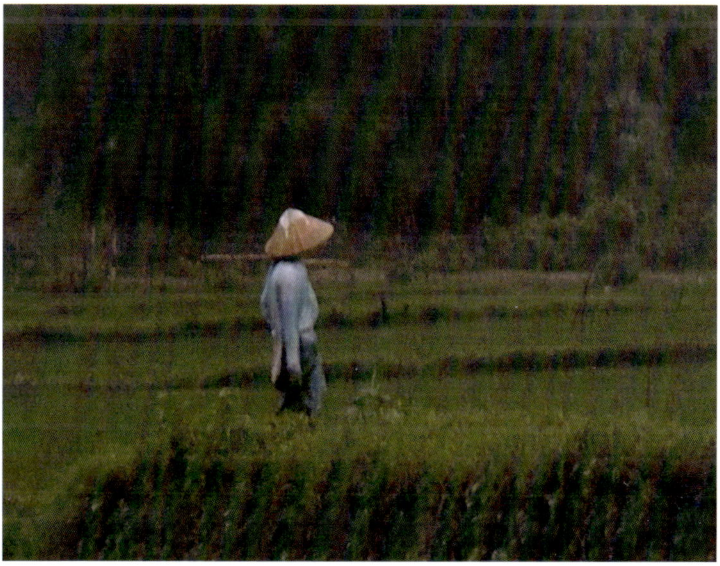

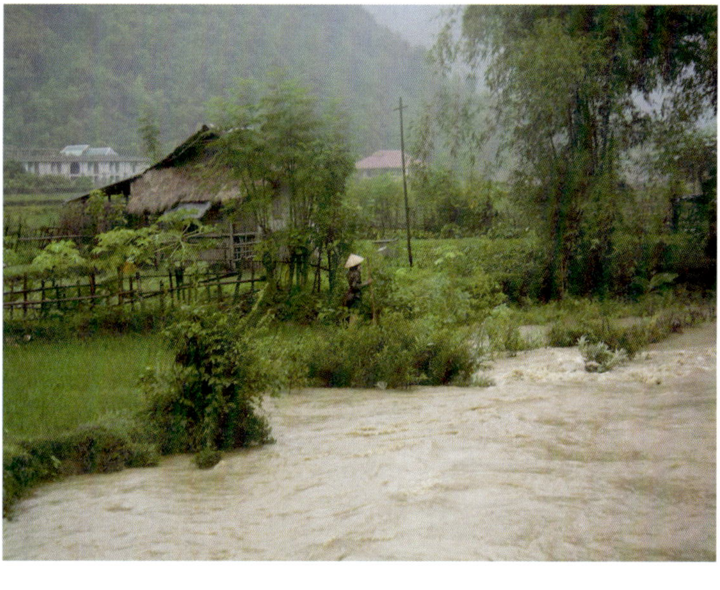

KATHLEEN HAMILTON

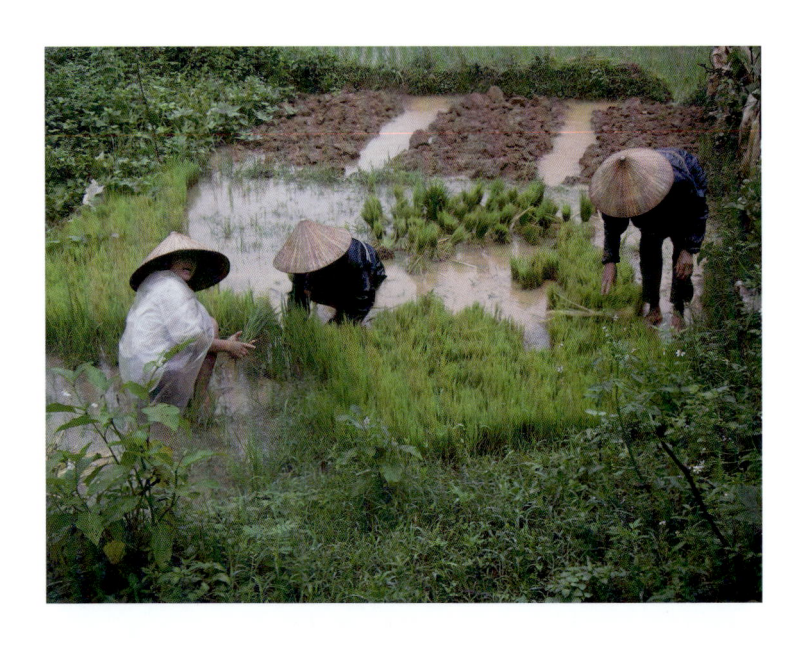

EDUCATING HA.NH

KATHLEEN HAMILTON

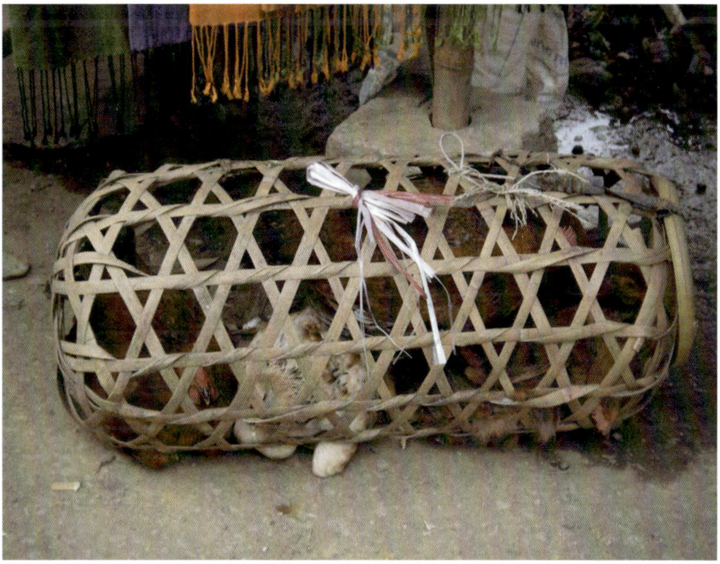

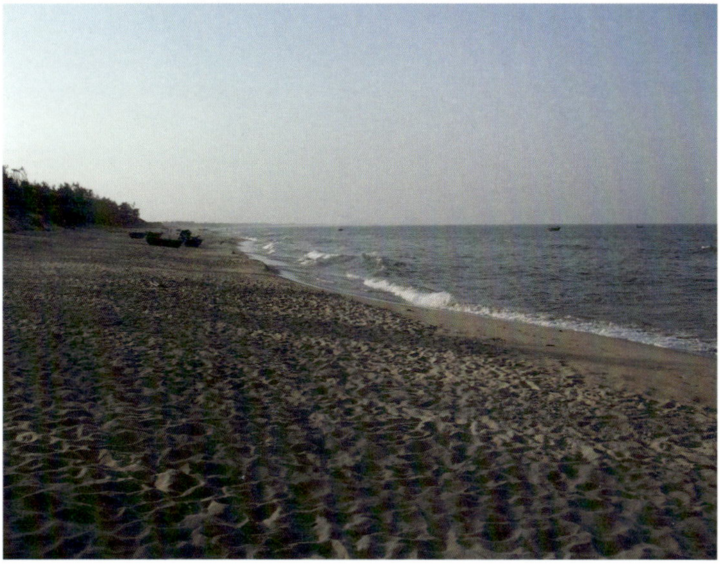

KATHLEEN HAMILTON

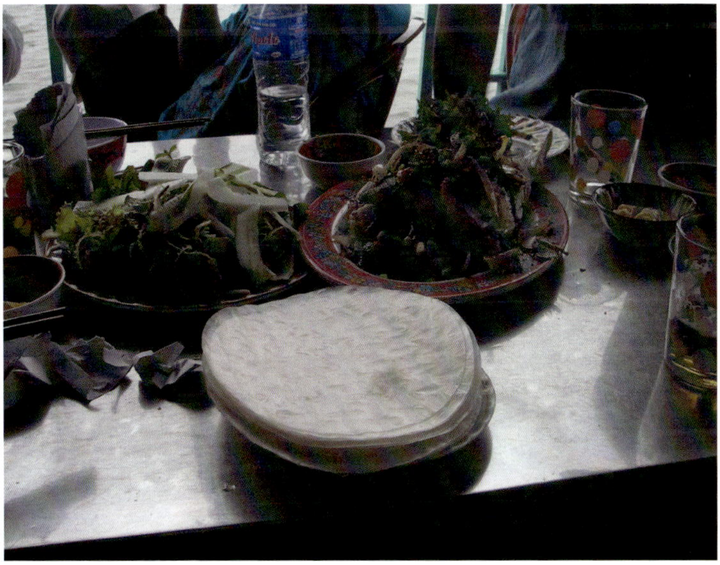

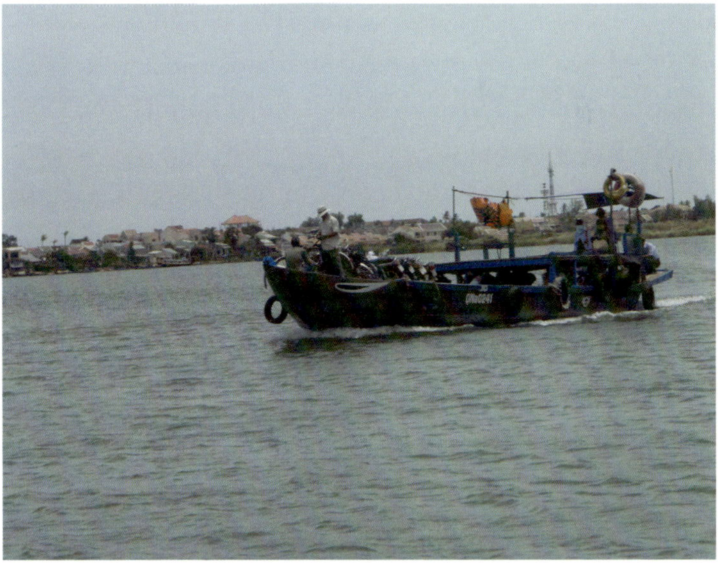

AS XUAN WAS BORN; a parallel on the other side of the world...

Xuan was born to a girl the same age as I was in 1973. Fourteen, she was only fourteen! My mother had also passed on, although later in life, but that was the only similarity between Xuan and me, and we would not even know the other existed for over three decades. With my father I watched news reports covering the Vietnam War, and decided at that point to be a pacifist. As an adult I was well educated, married, a teacher, raised three well-educated children. We led lives of a happy upper middle class family in a developed country. Then in 2010 we took a family vacation, a trip that would open my complacent eyes and change everything. On a private tour of Vietnam spanning from the Mekong Delta in the south to Ha long Bay in the north, the experience was like sitting in a movie theatre, exciting the senses; sight, smell, taste, hearing, and touch, but the desire to touch more strengthened with each sensual moment. So, later that year, on my own, I returned with a new purpose in my heart. Blessed, having grown up privileged and well educated, I knew that the time had come to share with those who were less fortunate, those who could still only dream. I went online, did a bit of research, and signed up with a small non-governmental organization (NGO) called the Global Village Foundation (GVF) to teach English for a month at a rural school in Central Vietnam.

From my window seat on the plane I took in the mountains and terraced rice fields of the north, the seemingly endless rice paddies, and the dotted landscapes of villages connected by dirt roads. As the plane was about to land at Da Nang airport I glimpsed China Beach and found myself smiling, hands clenched in anticipation. Glancing once again at the itinerary I had received, I stared at forty-five, the number of children in my class, 35-38°C, the average temperatures for that time of year, the modes of transportation (motorbike, taxi and ferry) and the picture of the lovely quaint hotel at which I would be staying. From the airport I would take a taxi to the town of Hoi An. At least Hoi An was somewhat familiar; I had been there before. With my stomach knotted, the plane bounced twice on the runway, and came to a smooth stop. As I stepped off the plane an incredible blanket of heat enveloped me, there to stay. For the next month I sweated off four kilos, while the locals wore jeans and jean jackets; parkas if it was a cold evening, under 28 degrees. Cool comfort was only to be found in my air conditioned, cockroach infested, "deluxe" hotel room, although credit must be given to the hard working geckos (my welcome roomies) and the 128,000 dong a night price (roughly $8.00 Canadian).

On Saturday, I was woken by an early morning knock and the eyes of a girl no more than nine years old. "Lady, clean room," she said, and not in the form of a question. That became the start of every day. As I arose every morning and prepared for the day I got to know little Lan well. Her mother worked at the hotel front desk. Every Monday morning they drove into town by moto, their term for motorbike, and worked until night time. Every Friday they drove back out to the village. When asked where they slept she told me they slept at the hotel. They certainly did, for one morning I arose earlier than usual, up with the setting-up of market stalls at five AM. There were Lan and her mother on the hotel lobby floor, apparently their other job was to be the night watch.

Monday morning I was up at six for I was to teach from 8:00-11:00, and then 2:00-4:00. A three hour lunch, to me, seemed excessive. I was to meet my GVF hosts in the lobby at 6:30. From there we would go for breakfast and drive to the school, by moto of course. With two 2-cubic foot boxes and a large bag full of donated materials from home (colouring books, crayons, writing tools, geometry sets, balls, and scribblers) I watched as my two hosts balanced these, me and themselves on two motos and off we went. We drove to a lovely restaurant across from the ferries and ate wonderful baguettes with cheese, reflecting a lovely French influence. The ferries were not the North American version, most likely not to be considered sea worthy here. Nonetheless they held roughly twenty motorbikes and thirty passengers at rush hour. I was further astounded after breakfast, for this was to be our second mode of transport every morning to school; two minutes to breakfast, seven minutes to cross the river, and then ten minutes along beautiful country roads dividing rice fields, to the school.

The quaint and inviting village school was a typical rural school of Vietnam, yellow, two-storied, with outdoor entrances, this one blessed with a grass field, as opposed to the usual concrete. I was to learn that the upkeep of the grounds was the responsibility of the students. They hand cut the grass with their small sickles from home, and cleaned the grounds. Of this they were proud. As we passed through the gate my stomach again lurched in anticipation. Summer holidays were almost over, except for those children who wanted to learn English. How much I could teach them over the period of a month was questionable, plus how much had they already been taught? I had so many questions, and soon to be, so many answers. I was awoken from my ramblings as I stepped into the classroom, for there in front of me were forty-five uniformed student standing saying, "Good morning teacher!"

"Good morning students!" I replied. There they were; not the five to seven year olds that I had been expecting, but ten to twelve year olds. I counted thirty-one girls and fourteen boys. In the cramped, already swelteringly hot classroom, full of double wooden desks and bench seating (in some cases occupied by three children), the class was eager to learn. And then I saw her, a girl much smaller than the rest, but I thought that she might just be very small. I wrote on the board "My name is Miss Kat" and introduced myself, followed by the introduction of each of my hosts, and then so on, row by row, through the class. These glorious forty-five foreign names were then written by each student on a piece of paper, which was then folded and put on the desks. The walls of the classroom were yellow and bare. I asked my hosts why there was no decoration in the classrooms other than a picture of Ho Chi Minh, and they replied that the government had decreed that any adornment on the walls would deter from the students' learning; a problem that I would remedy that very day. So, out came the crayons, and ninety eyes stared. I had the students draw their homes and families, and at the end of this exercise there were forty-five homes with rice fields, water buffalos, and families. I told the students to put the crayons in their desks and they became their treasures. Next was a lesson in art applique. Tape does not work on cement walls!, or so I learned. After a morning of falling art and retaping, I was exhausted, ready for lunch, a three hour lunch! That would give us time to go back into town and get some things done, preparations for the following day, shopping, etc. My hosts thought differently. "Why do that?" they asked. "We go to nice restaurant by river and relax. Have beer." I sighed under my breath and agreed. I am not sure who actually learned more, my students or me. Lunch was bliss. We sat over the river at a creaky restaurant, eating fresh snails, river prawns and fish, drinking beer, and relaxing. I watched men with their nets in the river, children riding bicycles, running errands, and sitting in the shade of a tree eating fresh mango. Women nursed and rocked their babies in hammocks. In their simple lives these people were in what seemed to me, still an outsider, like bliss.

As we ate I asked about the little one. "Wait," I said, "Ha.nh. Is that right?"

Vinh and Hung were very impressed, as was I, except that I could not remember any of the others. "Ha.nh," said Vinh, "very special girl."

"Why?" I asked.

"She only eight year old" replied Vinh. "Village fortune teller say she very good luck, very smart. Someday she be famous. So now that why she in your class. Her parents very proud."

There was obviously a lot for me to learn about this amazing culture. As the lunch hours ended I remembered the hanging pictures disaster and asked if we could get some string and clothes pegs.

"Easy" said Mr. Hung and he walked out of the restaurant, returning five minutes later with string and a package of clothes pegs.

"Good morning Miss Kat!" was my greeting as I entered the classroom.

"Afternoon. It is afternoon now. Good afternoon students" I said. And after tying the string to the window bars on either side of the classroom, on which to hang the pictures, the rest of the afternoon was spent studying numbers and reading the clock, the only other item on the echoing walls, and playing a wild outdoor game of "What Time is it, Mr. Crab?"

As I fell into my room after an amazing dinner I thought "I love this place!" and promptly fell asleep with my shoes on. An hour later I was woken by a knock on my door, a gentle knock I recognized as Lan's. "Mr. Vinh here see you Miss Kat." I fumbled for my phone to check the time. It was 8:00 PM. I looked out but no one was there. As she read my thoughts Lan said "he downstairs, wait for you." "OK, I will be right down" I said, and to that Lan bounded back down the three flights of stairs. As I stepped down the last step Mr. Vinh motioned for me to come with him. We got onto his moto, driving the two blocks to the local bar, the Tam Tam, the best in town. As we sat and sipped mojitos and Tiger Beer we discussed the day. "Class really like you!" said Mr. Vinh with a smile. "Tomorrow special day. We take mobile library to school so children have book to read. Then we go for special lunch at Xuan's house. Xuan Ha.nh's mother. Remember Ha.nh?" Of course I remembered Ha.nh. Mr. Vinh went on to say that Ha.nh's parents were very excited to talk to me, wanting me to teach Ha.nh to read and write very well. I did not know what to say, let alone what to expect, but felt very honoured to be invited

After a few beers, a few games of pool, and a dead sleep of five hours, 6:00 AM came early. However, today was to be a special day. I showered and was down stairs at 6:30 AM sharp, learning another lesson; in Vietnam on time had a two hour window! Fortunately my hosts had been taught by their employer to shrink that window to ten-minutes-max for foreigners. The morning routine was the same; watching the ferries embarking and disembarking, crossing the river, the activation of the senses; sight and smell, and "Good morning Miss Kat". 8:00-11:00 flew by, teaching the verb to be; "I am, he is, she is…", and the delivery of the mobile library. Eyes beamed, after each child chose a Vietnamese book, silent reading time was bliss, the children sitting under trees, on the school porch benches, lying on their tummies on the soft grass. After silent reading they each signed out a book, and it was lunch time. Books were taken home by excited children to show their parents, and read to younger siblings.

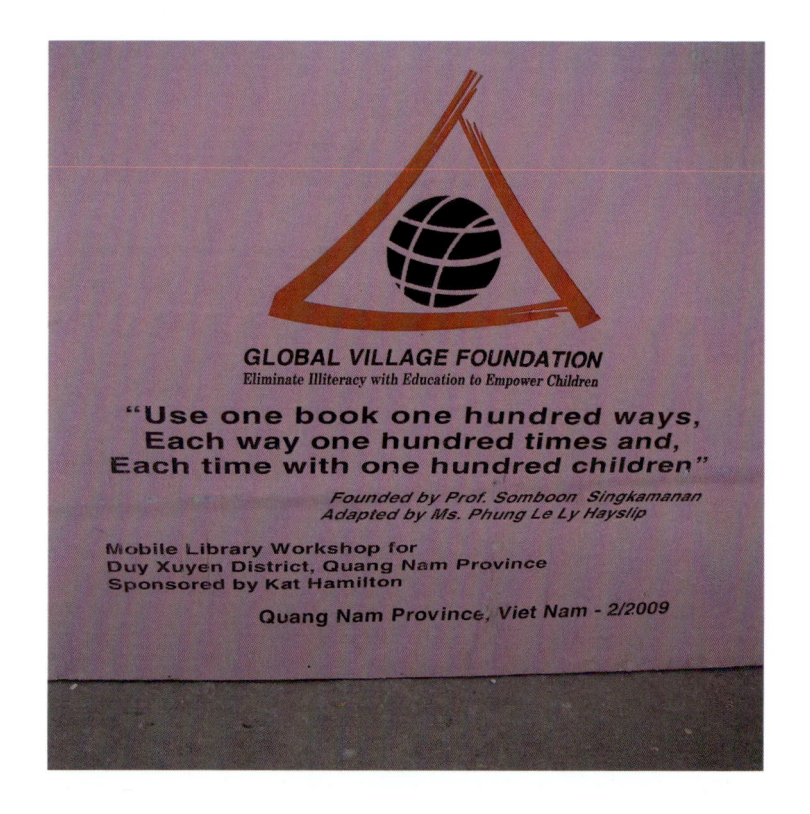

GLOBAL VILLAGE FOUNDATION
Eliminate Illiteracy with Education to Empower Children

"Use one book one hundred ways,
Each way one hundred times and,
Each time with one hundred children"

Founded by Prof. Somboon Singkamanan
Adapted by Ms. Phung Le Ly Hayslip

Mobile Library Workshop for
Duy Xuyen District, Quang Nam Province
Sponsored by Kat Hamilton

Quang Nam Province, Viet Nam - 2/2009

Lunch time, and at Ha.nh's house enough food to feed my entire class was laid on the floor, with sitting mats neatly spread. We were in a neatly kept small house on stilts overlooking the family rice field. Dishes of tom xao (stir fried sweet shrimp), muc xao (stir fried squid), pho (broth soup with noodles), ga roti (roasted chicken bits), papaya salad, white rice, fried rice, and spring rolls. As everyone gathered at the table introductions were made. Fortunately for me, my trusty translators, Mr. Vinh and Mr. Hung were seated next to me, for no one else at the table, other than Ha.nh spoke English. Altogether there were twelve of us; Ha.nh, her two brothers, Mot and Hai, Xuan and her husband Tuan, a school district official, the school principal and his secretary, Mr. Vinh, Mr. Hung, myself, and Xuan's mother Co^ng, the words of whom unravel in my mind still today. She told me her story, the story of her village, just a few kilometres from where we were sitting, her dreams and those of her sister, the war, of them and the other ones. I wanted to cry, to console, to carry Ha.nh, the little one carrying the weight of the family's honour on her shoulders because of the words of the village fortune teller. But Ha.nh looked at me with her beautiful eyes with a strength and passion that was far beyond her years. Co^ng then explained to me that the council sitting at the table had met and decided that I was the one, the chosen one, chosen by them, to lead Ha.nh, to teach her, to mentor her, to be the one to make her famous. All I could think of was Hollywood, such a North American view. But then they went on, they wanted her to be educated, to be able to read and do business, to go further than the Grade 5 average literacy level of her village. She was to be the one able to work in the city, Hoi An, or maybe even Da Nang. They wanted her to open a shop, a real shop. They showed me the beautiful weavings done by Ha.nh's tiny hands, ways taught to her by her mother and grandmother.

So that night I sat in silence, interrupted only twice by my gecko roomie named Ban, my friend following close behind a juicy cock roach. "What," I asked him, "can I accomplish in just over three weeks?" That day overtook me and through a restless night I dreamt interwoven images of the village, of war, of my students, of Ha.nh and her family, and of the beach I had been longing to see, but not yet seen. Along the beach ran Ha.nh, away from her grandmother, her natural grandmother, towards me, stopping and crying at my feet. Her mother disappeared but her voice came to me as a whisper, "feed her our dreams" she said, sweeping Ha.nh and I to the top of a mountain overlooking her village, sitting under an avocado tree reading. On closer inspection the mountain was not of soil and rock, but of books, a dishevelled library. And I was woken by the books tumbling, crashing down, with a loud rumble, becoming a soft knock. A single eye peered into my door with a stream of light. "Miss Kat, must come. You late for work" came Lan's voice. What day was it? Saturday, I was sure it was Saturday. No school today. "Five minutes…" was all my dream filled brain was able to come up with before hopping in for a cold shower.

As I reached the bottom of the stairs my hosts and another woman I did not recognize waited in the lobby. I was introduced to Miss Le Ly, founder of the NGO I was working for. This was an unexpected visit and I was thrilled. But before I was able to let my mind wander I was told that we were going to deliver mobile libraries to a neighbouring village school. As I climbed into the van, anticipating the wonderful smell of breakfast coming from inside, my heart skipped, for there was sitting Ha.nh who, it turned out, was to be my buddy for the next three weeks; my shadow. I was thrilled, replayed my dream, and I smiled. Then we ate, Hoi An style subs, *ban mai*, made fresh that morning, and ice coffee which I became dependent on to get me through the sweltering days. After forty-five minutes of panoramic scenes we stopped at a school similar to the one I taught at, but void of trees and grass, surrounded by concrete. "This school" said Miss Le Ly "is special. It has an empty lot next to it. I want donations to buy it and build an English teacher training centre, or maybe a women's trades centre." As I took this in, there came the voices of many children, and our day there began.

Also with us that day was Miss Oil from Thailand, a wonderful inspiration, and great friend-to-be. We were to become the two key players of the GVF workshops, held twice each year, over the next few years. Miss Oil was taught in university by Somboon Singkamanan in Bangkok. She had been taught to "Use one book one hundred ways, each way one hundred times and each time with one hundred children", a quote adapted by Miss Le Ly, written on each mobile library book box. Miss Oil brought books to life through drama and expression. I was the teacher of the teachers, bringing the classroom to life through questions, games, songs, and creativity. And to tie our teaching together were the mobile libraries.

And then, there was Ha.nh. The children saw that Ha.nh was different, for she was with Miss Kat, the teacher who came by airplane from across the world to teach them. Children looked up to her, and sat under the lone tree to listen to her read stories. At break time all of the children signed out a book from the book box and read, to themselves, to little brothers and sisters, to teachers with great pride. I realized that these children had gone through school without libraries of any kind and the only printed materials they were able to read were the rare text book, teachers' writings and propaganda. They were starved of this luxury that we often take for granted. At that moment I knew that this was where I was meant to be, where Ha.nh was meant to be, and that we were now intertwined. Without words, but rather through the joy we were experiencing, we both knew what the outcome of this would be.

As our team sat together on the beach that evening, watching the sun setting, listening to children at play and fishermen at work, feasting on freshly caught clams, we shared our interwoven dreams of that day, and for the future. I shared my restless dreams of the night before, and was told their purpose was to guide my future. I agreed and we planned for the teaching centre; the whens whys and whos of the centre, a grand plan needing large donations. We would have to get to work right away. And then a soft whisper came to us. It was that of Ha.nh, who had been silent through our sixty minutes of scheming, "I want to teach there. I want to teach weaving and English there when I grow up!" And there it was, laid before us all. Little Ha.nh who bore the weight of the world for her family would be famous, not only for the benefit of her family, but for that of Quang Nam Province, Central Vietnam.

My first promise was to purchase the land to build this dream. The key was then to find the volunteers and donors to build the mountain of books, the library, and the trades centre. Women would have the opportunity to become self-sufficient through literacy, and training. Their societal placement would change, they would become empowered.

CONCLUSIONS

Ha.nh was created to represent the impact female literacy can have on a community, from local to global. The pebble hits the water, and the ripples are far reaching. Statistics can be deceiving, and I believe that primary level literacy is no longer enough to empower anyone to succeed. I believe that an experience is worth a thousand words. Facts and figures on paper are a catalyst that can lead to either an understanding, or a need to seek understanding, but first hand experiences are a way in which empowerment can be achieved and perpetuate change for a brighter future; rooting in the home and spanning to the global family.

I believe it is not acceptable to sit on the pedestals of developed countries and dictate what needs to be done in developing countries, without experiencing the terrain while walking in their shoes. Without understanding their history, and their knowledge bases, how are we to instigate change for the better? Vietnam has a rich history, filled with feuds, battles, female warriors, matriarchal customs, Confucianism versus Buddhism, colonization, influences by China, France, the USSR, and the USA, communism versus democracy, strengthening its role in the global economy, and a determination for independence. Through all of this there was the struggle over the changing face of women.

From my personal experiences I saw that female empowerment is possible through literacy. If women show that they can think and reason both within and beyond the home setting, they gain power, status, and their hopes and dreams can advance further toward realities. The rural populous is often the one to suffer when government funding and resources are already scarce. This is where NGOs come in to take up the slack until the country is able to stand on its own. The work of NGOs reaches further; listening to the hopes and dreams of the people, witnessing injustices, and working to empower women. From my standpoint, working with GVF, empowerment is working. We are not able to empower all women, but for those few we are able to access, those who are willing to reach for their dreams, it is both rewarding and satisfying to provide assistance to aid in making it a reality. From Ha.nh to Ha.nh, through the generations, there is a common thread in the desires of women, desires of empowerment and hope for their next generation. As the country evolved, opening to western influences, these desires began approaching an achievable reality. In this case the rippling effects of Hanh, and Global Village Foundation, have rooted empowerment for her family, her community, and so on…. If we can empower one woman in a community then we have set the stage for putting a new standard in motion.

Printed in Canada